INTRODUCTION TO ADULTHOOD

INSTRUCTORS GUIDE

INDEX

I. LESSON MODULE ORIENTATION

II. BENEFITS VS.REWARDS PGS. 1-10

  a. MODULE 1 LESSON 1 PGS. 1-5

  b. MODULE 1 LESSON 2 PGS. 6-11

III. MAKING GOOD DECISIONS PGS. 12-22

  a. MODULE 2 Lesson 1 PGS. 12-16

  b. MODULE 2 LESSON 2 PGS. 17-22

IV. RESULTS AND CONSEQUENCES PGS. 23-32

  a. MODULE 3 LESSON 1 PGS.23-28

  b. MODULE 3 LESSON 2 PGS 29-32

V. SELF AWARENESS PGS. 33-42

  a. MODULE 4 LESSON 1 PGS. 33-38

  b. MODULE 4 LESSON 2 PGS. 39-42

FOREWARD

In youth there are a great many things we are not taught. There are a great many conversations we do not get to have. Time flies by and soon we are of an age to provide for ourselves without the knowledge we would like to have. Challenges are presented to us as we meet new people, go new places and encounter new situations which we are not prepared for. As we face these challenges, we do not often understand until many years later that the people, places and situations are less difficult than learning how we can manage ourselves while facing life's challenges.

Introduction to Adulthood Instructors Guide and Workbook are developmental tools offered to, Counselors, Therapists and Parents in order to share with today's youth concepts for managing ourselves in daily challenges they may find themselves addressing. These functional solutions have been gleaned through the author's life experiences, consulting with professionals and assisting others in addressing their individual difficulties for over 20 years.

We all share a common existence interacting with each other in shared places and situations. As individuals, no one can define for us how to apply these principles for ourselves. By learning solutions to common difficulties, we allow ourselves to apply our individuality in a way that benefits ourselves and others.

Most adults recognize the need for youth to be able to enjoy being young. Responsibilities will come soon enough. With this in mind, let us all remember that they will not be young forever and it is our privileged responsibility to help prepare our youth for adulthood. By accepting the responsibility to think, understand and apply solutions to individual challenges we can improve the world around us one decision at a time. It is my sincere hope that the information you find here will help youth and adults cooperate for the benefit of those around us one person and one decision at a time.

Sincerely,

A. J. Caleb

Author of Introduction to Adulthood

ORIENTATION

COURSE DESCRIPTION:

The purpose of these materials is to:

- Introduce concepts common to many individuals
- Assist clients and students in identifying their individual challenges and forming new skills.

The program requires the ACTIVE PARTICIPATION of another person working with the student or client.

Each Topic Module is divided into four sections intended to assist the Parent, Consultant or Counselor with differing approaches to communicating the subject matter. What amount of any section used depends on the participant's needs and maturity.

1. The Body of the Subject Matter is the basis for the concept being communicated and is meant to be utilized in all applications of the material.
2. Pictures contained within the modules are intended as interactive activities to identify examples of the concept being discussed.
3. Sidebar quotations and reflections provide expanding perspectives for discussion of how the subject matter relates to human development, religious and philosophical thought in most cultures throughout history.
4. Assignments are intended to encourage thought and reflection from simple examples of the subject.

The example on the next pages will assist in familiarizing yourself with the format each lesson will follow.

MAKING GOOD DECISIONS

EVERYTHING STARTS WITH A DECISION

At the point we begin being responsible for ourselves we also begin making decisions that affect the rest of our lives. If we are responsible in choosing things that benefit us, we produce benefits that can be appreciated by others. **By making good decisions we can satisfy our greatest needs in life.**

WHY DO WE MAKE DECISIONS?

We make decisions to satisfy our needs. If we chose to apply ourselves in school it likely earned us the respect of our parents, teachers and friends. Whether it was in academics or sports, that respect was a reward that likely produced the further reward of opportunities we could choose to be a part of. The rewards of respect and opportunity satisfy a desire that exists within every person to be appreciated and have hope for the future. Similarly, every decision we make is meant to satisfy a need.

WHO IS RESPONSIBLE FOR MAKING DECISIONS?

What we choose to do each day determines whether or not we get the respect and opportunity that satisfies our desires. What we choose to do each day also determines whether or not we continue to receive the appreciation from others that produces opportunities. As adults we must consider that each other adult is responsible to provide for themselves the basic necessities of life. If they are to be well respected and appreciated by others, each adult must be able to provide for themselves in the same way. Respect is the result of not creating a burden upon others to provide for us what we can and should provide for ourselves. Like

den to

with the

r ourselves

will grow

apable of

ern for their

That Security

and Peace creates the opportunity for us to receive the benefits of our parents Respect and Appreciation.

As adults we must make a decision of what we will do with the opportunities we have each day. What we choose to do with those opportunities will determine whether we create benefits within our lives or have a life full of things that produce no benefits.

Religious and philosophical quotes are chosen to be all inclusive of possible beliefs. Reflections are intended as opportunities to expand discussion of the topic. The combination of all 4 module sections is intended to encourage a maturation of thought as the student or client progresses through the subject matter.

"A GOOD MAN OUT OF THE GOOD TREASURE OF HIS HEART BRINGS FORTH GOOD…"

The Book of Luke 6:45

It can often seem that while we believe we are good people, we find ourselves surrounded by difficulties interacting with others. It is not possible to control the choices other people make. Before we decide others are at fault we must examine our own decisions. It is not enough for a decision to benefit us. We must consider how our decisions affect others.

In each lesson an example will be followed by questions intended to provoke thought by the student or client. As the responses are intended to create individual answers based on individual perspective, the preferred method of examining the answers is to accept the perspective of the student or client while promoting the principles in the lesson in a way the individual student or client will be able to accept.

EXAMPLE 2 QUESTIONS:

1. Have you ever had a reward that was made possible by something someone else did for you? What was it?____

2. In a few words, describe the reward you have received and the benefit you received from that reward.____

3. In a few words describe a benefit you have received and any rewards or benefits it made possible.

Questions to ask during instruction:

- Are the concepts discussed of value to the individual's personal development and growth?
- Are the concepts within the material communicated clearly?
- Is the Material presented in a format that is easily applicable to your understanding and experiences?

What you bring to the course material is your personal life experience. As an instructor you should familiarize yourself with each lesson and add your own experiences in discussion of the subject being discussed.

Each module will end assignments with a topic assignment that asks the student to demonstrate their understanding of the subject discussed. These assignments help the instructor to form an understanding of the student or client. These are also useful as something the instructor can refer to as a reflection for the student or client to examine their own thoughts.

TOPIC ASSIGNMENT

Write 3-4 paragraphs (3-5 sentences each) describing in your own words why we seek to earn rewards, the difference between rewards and benefits and which you think is more desirable to have.

It is often helpful to use different approaches in order to communicate a subject. Each module is followed by a collection of statements contained within the text of the module and formed to communicate the essential core of the subject matter. An instructor may wish to use one or all of the assignments or discussion tools as they feel necessary.

BOLD REALITIES

FOR DISCUSSION

At an early age we form an image of ourselves based on the level of respect we receive from others.

As we mature through life we continue to develop along these same lines. The goals we set for ourselves as rewards are chosen for the benefit we feel from having earned past rewards.

In looking back at the generations of our families we can identify how each person has adhered to the roles and responsibilities modern life has required of them. We have been taught by our experiences within society what to want and how we must earn it. We have been educated to demonstrate our individual worth to others by promoting ourselves and this puts each of us in conflict with everyone who has been taught to do the same thing.

In each of these circumstances conflict exists. The conflict in these situations is not created by the circumstances as much as it is created by our perspective.

If we take a moment to pause, most of us may realize the greatest benefits we can have in life are Peace and Security. Both rewards and benefits are produced by making good decisions. Rewards produce benefits that fade quickly. We simply need to choose whether the Peace and Security we desire for ourselves and others are produced by rewards we earn or benefits we create for ourselves and others.

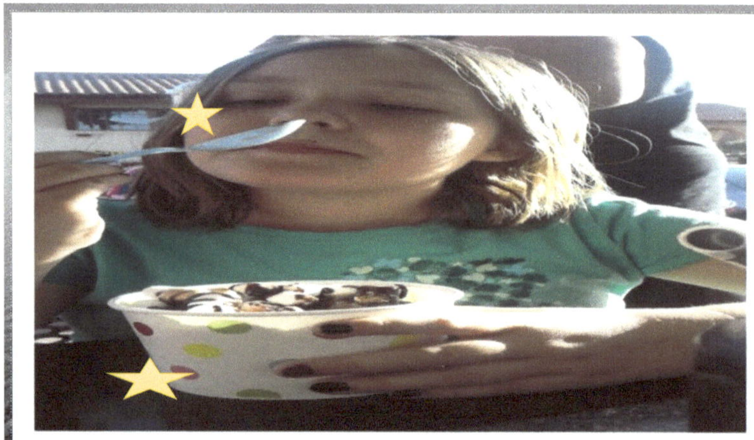

BENEFITS VS. REWARDS

BENEFITS BRING LONG TERM REWARDS. REWARDS DO NOT BRING LONG TERM BENEFITS.

Today benefits and rewards are incorrectly considered to be the same thing. Many of us develop habits that bring occasional rewards and develop cycles of behavior that keep us from recognizing the benefits we might have every day. We often find ourselves fully occupied with the day to day involvement of school, work and family while dreaming of a vacation. We purchase beverages like Coffee, Soda or Dinner Out as little rewards for making it through the week. When we do this we feel a level of satisfaction and enjoyment that comes from our reward for a job well done. Before too long that satisfaction and enjoyment can fade leaving us seeking another reward. Many of us find also ourselves unsatisfied after giving ourselves little rewards. This may be because our society has misplaced the difference between benefits and rewards. We often view them as the same thing. We view rewards as the beneficial result of doing something. A benefit is actually the positive result produced by a particular action while a reward is given based on the requirement of completing a particular action. A benefit will always be produced. A reward can be unavailable or taken away. This does not mean rewards are bad. The joy we feel from getting a reward is a real and valuable benefit of earning a reward. However, learning to recognize the difference between benefits and rewards gives us the opportunity to produce both rewards and benefits in our lives. When we realize that benefits produce rewards as well as other benefits that cannot be earned: we give ourselves the opportunity to enjoy larger, more meaningful rewards that benefit ourselves and others.

THE PICTURE:

The picture is intended to be discussed with the student (Following reading of the introductory paragraph and the sections titled What is a reward? & What is a Benefit?).

Each star designates an element of the picture to be discussed.

Questions to ask the student:

1. Does the girl in the picture seem to be enjoying the Frozen Yogurt?
2. How can you tell?
3. Is that enjoyment a benefit or a reward?
4. Does the frozen yogurt seem to have a lot of toppings?
5. Do you think the Frozen Yogurt is a reward for something the girl did?
6. Is there anything in the picture that defines the Frozen Yogurt as a reward?
7. Is it possible that a trip to the Froyo spot was simply a benefit of her parents love?

It is easy to define a benefit of having received something. How we define the difference between benefits and rewards depends on our individual perspective. The Frozen Yogurt was something the girl saw as a reward for being a good kid. Her father bought it for her to see the benefit of happiness in her life. The Frozen yogurt was a benefit of his love. The child was focused on a reward. The adult focused on producing a benefit of happiness for both of them.

BENEFITS VS. REWARDS

MODULE 1: LESSON 1

BENEFITS VS. REWARDS

BENEFITS BRING LONG TERM REWARDS. REWARDS DO NOT BRING LONG TERM BENEFITS.

What is a reward?

The most common example of reward vs. benefit is the money received for work completed in an occupation. A job is given to be done and when it is completed pay is received by the worker. Like all rewards, receiving pay for work is a positive experience. Pay allows the employee to purchase what they need to live. It also requires the employee to return to work in order to get payed again. If the job no longer exists or is not completed to the satisfaction of the employer; the money received by the worker may not be available in the future.

Money is the reward for work and the benefit it creates depends completely on how it is spent by the worker. Money itself is simply an object we give value to so we can buy things. We enjoy being payed but if we lose our money at a casino there is nothing it has produced of any benefit. If we win more money at a casino, we feel excited but we are still left only with an object we must decide how to use.

What is a Benefit?

Benefits are positive results that are produced for ourselves and others by our responsible choices and actions. If we go to work we will receive pay but if we apply ourselves to our trade we gain the benefits of experience, knowledge and the respect of others which often leads to greater pay. Likewise, if we choose to spend the money we make to pay our bills we may have the rewards of a home that gives shelter, a car so we aren't walking and food to eat. Comfort and enjoyment that can be shared with others are gained as benefits. Benefits can also be found from choices and actions that have no immediate reward. If our home remains unclean, we will spend time searching for things we need to work, cause ourselves to be late and risk the reward of pay we might receive. If our home remains clean, we will have the benefit of knowing where things are when we need them and the peace of being able to restfully prepare for work. The person who arrives to work early and rested is available and ready to gain the experience, knowledge and respect of others who can rely on that person to do their job. These benefits lead to greater pay. Benefits always lead to greater rewards.

THE READING:

Time should be allotted for cooperative reading of the subject material. Engaging the student actively reading in a shared environment requires the student to participate vocally and actively listen.

PRINCIPLE BEHIND THE READING:

Whether or not the student works, the concept of working is known to everyone. What a person chooses to do with money earned determines whether their efforts at work produce any benefits. People often think they work for money and try to earn as much as they can but we actually work to gain the benefits of security and enjoyment we receive from how we spend our money.

QUESTIONS:

1. Can you think of a time when there was not much money to buy things needed?
2. Can you remember if things felt unhappy or stressful at that time?
3. Can you think of a time there was not much money to do things but you had everything you needed?
4. Did things feel as stressful or unhappy?

SUGGESTED ACTIVITY:

Prior to reading and discussing the picture, provide the student with an enjoyable snack or beverage. After reading and discussion ask the student if there was any reward involved in what they received.

BENEFITS VS. REWARDS

MODULE 1: LESSON 1

WISDOM IS THE PRINCIPLE THING; THEREFORE GET WISDOM. AND IN ALL YOUR GETTING, GET UNDERSTANDING.

The Book of Proverbs 4:7

Wisdom is the ability to apply knowledge in the best way possible for any given situation. Many of the decisions we make have no rule or requirement to guide them. We may feel a decision effects no one but ourselves. Wisdom is applied by looking at the results of our decisions with the understanding of how our decisions affect others as well as ourselves.

NOTES: **PERSONAL EXPERIENCES**

____

____

____

____

____

____

____

____

____

____

____

____

____

____

____

____

____

____

USE OF SCRIPTURE:

Because a young adult attends church with their parents does not mean they necessarily believe in their parents religious beliefs. Because a particular faith may be judged harshly by opinion does not mean it is without value. Regardless of a student's religious beliefs or lack of religious beliefs, attention needs to be drawn to the role of religion, science and philosophy throughout history. Our beliefs help us understand the elements of living that exist beyond the events we experience. Each belief system that exists attempts to give wisdom and understanding of how to attain the benefits we all desire beyond what we physically experience.

DEFINITIONS:

Wisdom (wiz'dom): The quality of being wise; the power or faculty of forming the fittest and best judgement in any matter presented for consideration…

Understanding (un der stand'ing): Knowing, skillful, intelligent. The act of one who understands or comprehends; comprehension; apprehension and appreciation….that power by which we perceive, conceive and apprehend.

PRINCIPLE BEHIND SCRIPTURE:

In our youth wisdom and understanding are things we often assume will automatically develop as we grow older. When we are young we often think that we have gained wisdom and understanding simply by making decisions in our experiences as we become adults. However, we often meet adults who seem to have no wisdom or understanding. If wisdom and understanding were the result of each person developing them through their experiences: all adults would display wisdom and understanding.Wisdom and understanding do not come from simply experiencing things and making decisions.Wisdom is the ability to comprehend and appreciate the elements of a circumstance.Understanding is the ability appreciate and perceive how elements work together in a circumstance.

HOW THIS APPLIES TO BENEFITS AND REWARDS:

Earning or gaining rewards requires little or no application of Wisdom and Understanding. Earning a reward as an individual or within a group requires little or no thought as to how our decisions or the decisions of our group depend upon or affect anything outside of ourselves or a group we belong to. In sports we execute a game plan or individual strategy. In academics we study a subject and take a test. A reward is earned by an individual or group and is not shared by anyone else.

BENEFITS VS. REWARDS

WHY DO WE SEEK REWARDS?

In modern society most individuals have been conditioned to seek rewards. As children we are rewarded for completing our school work with a grade. In sports we are rewarded for winning with an award or trophy. In classes we are rewarded with honors and diplomas for work well done. We learn that each individual receives different rewards based on their performance. Because we learn that individuals are rewarded differently we also learn to compare ourselves to others based on the rewards we receive. These rewards may or may not earn us the respect, attention and affection of others.

Because individual rewards are different for each individual we each develop different goals for ourselves.

EXAMPLE 1:

Sally might not run as fast as Johnny but she may be faster than Billy. Johnny receives the award for being the fastest. Sally receives the award for being faster than the others but not as fast as Johnny. If Billy receives an award, it is one that distinguishes him as being not as fast as Johnny or Sally.

EXAMPLE 1 QUESTIONS:

1. In the spaces provided explain how you think Johnny, Sally and Billy feel about their performance and how their Coaches, friends and parents might respond to the race.

A. Johnny____

____

B. Sally____

____

C. Billy____

____

We all know that beyond the awards there is the respect we feel from others. **At an early age we form an image of ourselves based on the level of respect we receive from others.** In more recent times individual placement awards have often been replaced with participation awards to make the differences between individuals less significant in how children develop. However, among the children Johnny is still the fastest, Sally is still faster than everyone else and Billy may be considered the boy who lost to a girl if the other kids are mean.

MODULE 1: LESSON 1

PRINCIPLE BEHIND THE READING:

Having established the principles of applying wisdom and understanding in order to identify the difference between rewards and benefits; it is now necessary to apply wisdom and understanding to identify why we value rewards and benefits. Having emotional maturity means we can identify the shared experiences of individuals and appreciate the differences of how rewards and benefits are experienced by individuals.

SUGGESTED ACTIVITY:

Have the student briefly relate a childhood experience of having earned a reward explaining how it made them feel.

ASSESSING STUDENTS EXAMPLE 1 ANSWERS:

There are no right or wrong answers to example 1 questions.

SUGGESTED ACTIVITY:

Have the student read the paragraph below the answer and explain how their answers relate to what is said. If the student's answers do not relate: Ask if the student can explain how someone with different experiences than theirs might relate to what is written in the paragraph.

BENEFITS VS. REWARDS

MODULE 1: LESSON 1

As we mature through life we continue to develop along these same lines. If Johnny remains the fastest and continues to receive awards, he may devote himself completely to a sport involving speed. This would bring the involvement of coaches and teammates with the encouragement and training they offer. If Sally continues to perform and receive awards as she did, she may continue to run for enjoyment and focus on another interest she performs well in. Her performance may not cause her to continue racing but she has the experience of having done well to apply confidence in other areas. If Billy continues to perform as he did, it is not likely that he will continue to focus on running. He may choose to pursue another interest or choose to pursue nothing. There will be no encouragement from coaches, no support of teammates and no experience that breeds confidence for Johnny. If the respect he feels from others becomes nonexistent he may lose motivation for anything.

The goals we set for ourselves as rewards are chosen for the benefit we feel from having earned past rewards. Studies have proven that if Johnny, Sally or Billy apply themselves to something they feel supported and respected for; they are likely to continue in the activity without a trophy or award. This is because we seek rewards to gain the benefits they might produce if we perform well. Ultimately the reward itself means very little if the benefits are not produced. We have been taught that the benefits of support, respect and affection must be earned through winning rewards.

HAVEN'T THINGS ALWAYS BEEN THIS WAY?

In the earliest histories of humanity, hunter and gatherer societies had a far different existence from what we know in modern times. Tribes were families that found their needs supported and provided by their individual efforts, achievements and successes contributing to the Tribe as a whole. Whereas today people attempt to carve out their individuality independent of each other, the members of a tribe found their individuality defined by what they contributed to others. In the college textbook World History Before 1600: The Development of Early Civilization, the authors state: “Among hunter gatherers, survival of the group depends on the sharing of food collected into a common supply by all members, and all who contribute to the general store of food are valued equally, regardless of sex”. It was not until the development of Agriculture gave us the ability to settle in individual locations that the idea of individual possession of common needs arose. No longer living nomadic or constantly moving lives, women became primarily occupied with childbirth while men became occupied with the cultivating of food and livestock. As supplies of these items became more abundant, the ability of an individual to profit over his fellows began to be a reality. If a man could get his fellow tribe members to labor for his benefit; it increased the amount of common needs he could control within his tribe.

DISCUSSION OPPORTUNITY:

As children we never thought much of rewards until we saw another person earn one. The desire to earn a reward actually results from a comparing ourselves to someone who has already earned a reward. Ultimately the reward is something we identify ourselves as being equal to or better than others by earning. If what we truly desire is the sense of identity we gain from accomplishing something; how much sense does it make to identify ourselves by a reward we may not succeed earning in a competition?

SIGNIFICANCE OF HISTORY:

We do not concern ourselves with history as we conduct ourselves in our daily live but it is important to understand how history has developed to support structures of government and financial systems. The system of earning rewards supports stable governments and economies where millions of people from different backgrounds must co-exist and find ways to provide for their daily needs.

MATURE CONSIDERATION:

As adults we must accept without emotion that we have been taught to earn rewards but truly desire the benefits of respect and appreciation from others. We must accept that our desire for rewards does not come from a reward itself but how we identify ourselves by having earned it. Earning rewards supports an overall system in which we can exist peacefully with strangers. As adults earning rewards gains us the respect of strangers that share no personal connection to us. Each person earns rewards, returns home and lives with their friends and family. If what we desire in our homes are the benefits of love, respect and appreciation from those we care for, we must ask ourselves if earning rewards produces these benefits within our personal relationships and homes.

BENEFITS VS. REWARDS

MODULE 1: LESSON 2

HOW DOES THIS APPLY TO US TODAY?

Our modern realities are based in the development of our history as humans. Modern history has given us the development of governments and business built on the principles of individual achievement over our fellow man. **In looking back at the generations of our families we can identify how each person has adhered to the roles and responsibilities modern life has required of them.** As commercialization of everything from food to entertainment replaced individuals producing their own food and basic needs; we became dependent upon companies to earn money. The benefit of independence through individual labor was traded for the convenience of having someone else work in the dirt to produce our food. Modern conveniences such as a dishwasher or washing machine did not exist in many homes as recently as the 1950's. In recent decades it has become desirable and in most cases necessary for both parents within a home to work. Since the 1970's, rising costs of living and dependence on employment by companies has created the reality that a single working parent cannot provide the type of life most of us consider we deserve. With the rise of entertainers as Icons and informational ability to advertise wealth; large homes and luxurious cars have become what we expect to have as we mature to adulthood. **We have been taught by our experiences within society what to want and how we must earn it.**

Formalized education is one thing most of us have in common but it does not teach us how to live within our homes. **We have been educated to demonstrate our individual worth to others by promoting ourselves and this puts each of us in conflict with everyone who has been taught to do the same thing.** As we grow, we come to expect that the needs we have at home are the responsibility of our parents to provide. Reaching our teenage years, our desires for social activity and needs for greater independence often place us at odds with our parents due to this expectation. At this age, some of us feel that because we have earned achievements in school the respect we deserve entitles us to being given the reward of our needs being met. Many parents offer their children a car and insurance as a reward for good grades. Unless we understand that the car will become a tool we use to care for ourselves; we do not recognize the full independence our parents are preparing us for.

NOTES: **PERSONAL EXPERIENCES.**

____

____

____

THE READING:

The first paragraph of "How does this apply to us today?" is intended to pick up where Lesson 1 ended, recap the effects of History on how we view rewards and benefits and refocus the student on how this relates to the lives of individuals today.

QUESTIONS:

1. Ask the student to relate the traditional differences between men and women in the home.
2. Ask the student to explain whether or not those roles apply to life today?
3. Is life more expensive today?

As society changes, the roles society places on us change to meet cost of living. However, the requirement of working for the reward of money does not mean our personal lives will be happy.

COOPERATIVELY READ THE SECOND PARAGRAPH WITH STUDENT

QUESTIONS:

1. Is there an activity you were rewarded for doing as a child which you still complete but no longer receive a reward for doing?
2. Is there a benefit for completing that task without a reward?

As children we have been trained to expect a reward for doing things. As adults we must do these things for the benefits we receive from doing them.

BENEFITS VS. REWARDS

MODULE 1: LESSON 2

CHANGING PERSPECTIVES

When we transition into adulthood we are faced with the reality that we will not be living with our parents forever. This change in our realities can cause many of us conflict when it forces us to face our need to provide for ourselves. Many parents do not have the ability to offer cars and many of us struggle to meet our needs without knowing how. Many of us develop a desire to be independent thinking that without the authority of our parents we will enjoy a more carefree life. Some of us feel there is no reason we should have to provide for ourselves believing we will eventually provide for ourselves the same or better lifestyle they provide. Some of us have no choice and find there is no longer a home available for us with our parents.

In each of these circumstances conflict exists. Our fierce desire to be independent likely causes our parents to feel we do not appreciate what they provide. Those of us who feel this way may find they are moving into independence sooner than they are ready. Those of us who remain at home refusing to leave until we have the life we desire, likely find ourselves faced with the reality that our parents expect us to leave before we feel ready. For those who find themselves without the option of staying with their parents, there is no choice in the matter. Each of these situations share the perspective that what has been provided by our parents no longer exists as a reward for the achievements we have made. The care we have become accustomed to as a reward no longer produces the benefit of food and shelter. This is because we often mistake the care of others as a reward when it is actually a benefit that cannot be earned.

The conflict in these situations is not created by the circumstances as much as it is created by our perspective. Even if our parents offer us a vehicle for good grades, the ability for them to do so is the benefit of their work to earn money and their care for us. If our parents met every need and desire we had as children, it was a benefit of their work and care for us as well. If we find that our parents tell us they can no longer afford to feed and clothe us, it is possible that the reward of pay they receive for their work has changed. It is also possible that the benefit of their care is not appreciated by us remaining at home when we are at an age to work ourselves. We may realize everything we consider a reward was actually the benefit of care we received from our parents by considering this. When we realize the care we received from our parents is a benefit of their work or even just their legal responsibility, we should recognize that as adults we are not entitled to benefit of care from others.

What we expect of ourselves and what is expected of us by others changes:

1. As society changes
2. As the demands of life change.
3. As our responsibilities change from childhood to adulthood.

As individuals we feel conflict when what we expect is not received or what we were taught to expect no longer exists as a reward. What is expected of us and what we can reasonably expect for ourselves changes throughout life. However, we do not seem to feel conflict or question when what we desire for ourselves changes in the same way.

QUESTIONS:

1. Can you think of a TV character you wanted to be like when you were a small child?
2. Can you think of a famous person who's life you would like to have now that you are older?

When we stop to consider moments when we no longer received a reward that we had been taught to expect; we will find that it was not the reward we valued as much as the benefit we felt from having received the reward. No longer receiving a reward may have caused us to feel less loved, less worthy of receiving an award or simply less happy. Realizing this, we can identify benefits are actually more important to us than rewards.

BENEFITS VS. REWARDS

MODULE 1: LESSON 2

When a benefit we have received no longer exists we can feel challenged realizing our need to provide it for ourselves. In facing what we must do to provide for ourselves, a reality that we must work replaces our comfortable expectations. We once had the peaceful comfort of casually understanding these things were payed for by someone else. Food, shelter and comfort we did not often think about may suddenly not be easy to provide. Now we are faced with the decisions of which needs we must have in order to live as adults without being homeless. We become concerned with providing ourselves with a sense of security.

If we take a moment to pause, most of us may realize the greatest benefits we can have in life are Peace and Security. All other desires we may have are connected to providing ourselves with that greatest benefit. If Sally desires to color her hair she may not be sure what color she wants but definitely desires the security of feeling attractive. If Johnny wants a better physique he may not know what gym he will join but he knows he also wants the security of feeling attractive. Feeling secure in our desires gives us a sense of peace. In all things, as adults we want to return to a state of peaceful security knowing that our needs will be met.

NOTES: **PERSONAL EXPERIENCES.**

When we realize that we must provide things for ourselves we can be distracted by the conflict we feel. The conflict we feel is caused because we no longer feel Peace and Security knowing that what we desire will be readily available in the way we are used to. We may feel:

Mistreated: It may seem unfair for our responsibilities to suddenly change.

Lied to: What we have grown to expect can no longer be expected.

Unprepared: We may not understand how to provide for ourselves.

What we focus our attention on creates whether we feel conflict and disappointed feelings or:

A healthy challenge to learn how to provide ourselves with the Peace and Security we truly desire.

Any time we feel conflict, the natural human reaction is to re-create the same situations that previously existed when we felt Peace and Security. As children when things changed we:

Cried: The result of being emotionally overwhelmed and unable to communicate. (Ages 0-?)
Argued: The result of being emotionally overwhelmed and unable to communicate. (Ages 2-?)
Some adults never mature beyond this.

Developing maturity requires us to recognize that we do not actually desire a reward for doing things. Maturity requires recognizing we desire the Benefits of Peace and Security accepting we must learn to produce these benefits for ourselves. This is part of developing a mature perspective on life.

BENEFITS VS. REWARDS

MODULE 1: LESSON 2

HOW DO WE IDENTIFY A BENEFIT FROM A REWARD?

By examining the difference between benefits and rewards we can begin to recognize that peace and security are created by benefits.

EXAMPLE 2:

In high school a car gave Johnny the ability to drive Sally to Prom Night producing the benefit of memories and enjoyment for them both. Johnny worked to buy the car in high school and considered it the reward of his labor but as an adult he does not want to live in his car. If Johnny wants to earn money, the car now provides the benefit of transportation to work so he can afford to live. Johnny will have the benefit of security without worrying about transportation to work. The car may have been viewed as a reward when it was actually a benefit of being able to purchase a vehicle while Jonny lived with his parents. That benefit now provides Johnny the ability to earn the reward of pay that will continue as long as he has transportation to work.

Johnny had rewarded himself by purchasing an older sports car he liked. As an adult, Johnny now needs his car in order to work and maintaining an older car has become something he cannot afford. The enjoyment of driving his sports car is something Johnny has always enjoyed. However, beyond that enjoyment the car does not produce any further benefit for Johnny by being a sports car as it gets older. When the salesman at the car dealership saw Johnny drive in, she decided to show Johnny a new sports car. The price was higher than Johnny was planning on paying. In order to afford paying his other bills, Johnny wanted to pay a lot less each month. Johnny could choose to reward himself with the sports car which will make it difficult to afford his other bills. Johnny can also purchase another car that provides the long term benefit of peace and security in his ability to afford other things.

EXAMPLE 2 QUESTIONS:

1. Have you ever had a reward that was made possible by something someone else did for you? What was it?__________
2. In a few words, describe the reward you have received and the benefit you received from that reward.____________________
3. In a few words describe a benefit you have received and any rewards or benefits it made possible.____________________

Having established a mature understanding that:

> We have been taught by society to provide for our needs by earning rewards.
> We have been raised expecting that we receive rewards for doing well or maintaining our responsibilities.
> When we are faced with the conflict of providing ourselves with our own needs; our natural reaction is to recreate what we are familiar with in order to feel Peace and Security in our lives.

As adults we must be aware of how we may continue seeking to reward ourselves with what we may feel we deserve, desire out of the habit of seeking rewards and may not produce the benefits of Peace and Security we actually desire from our decisions.

We base many of our decisions in the feelings our past experiences created for us. Because of this, it is good to examine whether what we have considered rewards in our past were actually benefits provided to us.

Being aware of our:

1. Motivation to seek rewards
2. Natural tendency to identify ourselves by the rewards we might give ourselves
3. Responsibility to provide ourselves with our basic needs and desires
4. True desire for benefits rewards might produce more than rewards themselves

Allows us to apply understanding to the decisions we must make each day.

Actually making decisions that will provide us with the benefits of life we truly desire is the application of Understanding and Wisdom in choices that can be considered MATURE ADULT DECISIONS.

BENEFITS VS. REWARDS

MODULE 1: LESSON 2

TOPIC SUMMARY

Benefits and rewards result from decisions we make to experience the feelings we get from them. **Both rewards and benefits are produced by making good decisions.** However, decisions that produce benefits continue to produce benefits for ourselves and others. **Rewards produce benefits that fade quickly.** If we sell something of value it may give us the ability to buy something else. We will need to work or sell something else in order to gain that benefit again. If we make decisions to care for ourselves and others it provides more than just the reward of what was purchased. These decisions then produce the benefits of peace and security in our lives. The peace and security we provide for ourselves and others also removes many difficulties from our lives. The things we often decide to acquire as rewards for ourselves produce benefits that fade. When the benefit of a reward is gone we then seek another reward and can continue endlessly in this cycle. When our decisions produce benefits for ourselves and others, they continue to produce benefits that cannot be gained from any reward.

We simply need to choose whether the Peace and Security we desire for ourselves and others are produced by rewards we earn or benefits we create for ourselves and others.

TOPIC ASSIGNMENT

Write 3-4 paragraphs (3-5 sentences each) describing in your own words why we seek to earn rewards, the difference between rewards and benefits and which you think is more desirable to have.

____
____
____
____
____
____
____
____
____
____
____
____
____
____
____

The Topic Summary is a brief expansion into the next training module describing how decisions to seek rewards or benefits continue beyond the individual decisions we make and affect ourselves as well as others. The Topic Summary recaps the overall message of the subject material which is:

As adults we must choose to make decisions to seek rewards that fade or responsibly make decisions that will produce benefits for ourselves and others.

It may be helpful for the student to have the instructor read their Topic Assignment and discuss it with the student.

There are no correct answers to the topic assignment.

The Topic Assignment allows the instructor to gain a perspective of the students, thoughts feelings and opinions in order to establish a foundation for discussing the final portion of the Training Module.

Instructions for "BOLD REALITIES" section:

Bold Realities for Discussion are portions of the text which appear in **Bold Type** within the Training Module. It is suggested that the discussion of these principles be conducted in an informal manner. Discussing this portion casually reinforces the understanding of the subject material within the mind of the student. This forum allows that understanding to be freely expressed without the requirement of structured questions, answers or written assignments. It is suggested that each be discussed separately and within the context how they are combined.

BOLD REALITIES

FOR DISCUSSION

At an early age we form an image of ourselves based on the level of respect we receive from others.

As we mature through life we continue to develop along these same lines. The goals we set for ourselves as rewards are chosen for the benefit we feel from having earned past rewards.

In looking back at the generations of our families we can identify how each person has adhered to the roles and responsibilities modern life has required of them. We have been taught by our experiences within society what to want and how we must earn it. We have been educated to demonstrate our individual worth to others by promoting ourselves and this puts each of us in conflict with everyone who has been taught to do the same thing.

In each of these circumstances conflict exists. The conflict in these situations is not created by the circumstances as much as it is created by our perspective.

If we take a moment to pause, most of us may realize the greatest benefits we can have in life are Peace and Security. Both rewards and benefits are produced by making good decisions. Rewards produce benefits that fade quickly. We simply need to choose whether the Peace and Security we desire for ourselves and others are produced by rewards we earn or benefits we create for ourselves and others.

MAKING GOOD DECISIONS

EVERYTHING STARTS WITH A DECISION

At the point we begin being responsible for ourselves we also begin making decisions that affect the rest of our lives. If we are responsible in choosing things that benefit us, we produce benefits that can be appreciated by others. **By making good decisions we can satisfy our greatest needs in life.**

NOTES: **PERSONAL EXPERIENCES**

The picture is intended to be discussed with the student (Following reading of the introductory paragraph and the sections titled why do we make decisions? & Who is responsible for making decisions?).

Each star designates an element of the picture to be discussed.

Questions to ask the student:

8. Does the older girl seem aware of where they are walking? How can you tell?
9. Does the younger girl seem to feel safe?
10. Could the older girl be listening to music on her cell phone?
11. Do you think the older girls decisions provides both girls the opportunity to enjoy being together?

The opportunity to make good decisions happens in every decision we make each day. The little things we do provide ourselves and others the opportunity to have the benefits of Peace, Security, Respect, Appreciation, Happiness and Comfort.

Choices we make to be aware of the world around us, value the wellbeing of others and act responsibly allow us to be appreciated and removes unnecessary worry from the lives of those we love. These choices also allow us to experience things with others we might otherwise miss.

MAKING GOOD DECISIONS

WHY DO WE MAKE DECISIONS?

We make decisions to satisfy our needs. If we chose to apply ourselves in school it likely earned us the respect of our parents, teachers and friends. Whether it was in academics or sports, that respect was a benefit that likely produced the further benefit of opportunities we could choose to be a part of. The benefits of respect and opportunity satisfy a need that exists within each person to be appreciated and have hope for the future. Similarly, every decision we make is meant to satisfy a need.

WHO IS RESPONSIBLE FOR MAKING DECISIONS?

What we choose to do each day determines whether or not we get the respect and opportunity that satisfies those needs. What we choose to do each day also determines whether or not we continue to receive the appreciation from others that produces opportunities. As adults we must consider that each individual adult is responsible to provide for themselves the basic necessities of life. Each adult must be able to provide for themselves in the same way if they are to be well respected and appreciated by others. Respect is the result of not creating a burden upon others to provide for us what we can and should provide for ourselves. Like any benefit, it ceases to exist when the choices that created it cease to be made. When we become a burden to others respect given to us by others ceases to exist. Appreciation is the result of making decisions which produce benefits for ourselves and others. A parent's greatest hope is that their child will grow to be successful and healthy. To see a child become capable of providing for themselves replaces every parents concern for their child's wellbeing with a sense of Peace, Security, Happiness and Comfort. The creation of benefits in the lives of others creates the opportunity for us to receive the benefits of Respect and Appreciation that satisfies our own needs.

We must decide what we will do with the opportunities we have each day as adults. What we choose to do with those opportunities will determine whether we create benefits within our lives or have a life full of choices that produce no benefits.

NOTES: **PERSONAL EXPERIENCES.**

____

____

____

____

____

____

____

____

Time should be allotted for cooperative reading of the subject material. Engaging the student actively reading in a shared environment requires the student to participate vocally and actively listen.

As individuals we make decisions to satisfy our wants and needs. Because we are individuals, we do not often consider the wants and needs of others. However, as individuals we need the respect and consideration of others in order to satisfy our need to feel appreciated and valued by more than just ourselves.

QUESTIONS:

1. Have you ever received a gift from a friend for no apparent reason?
2. How did that make you feel?
3. How did it make you feel about the person who gave it to you?

By giving consideration to the needs of others which we all share as individuals, we create the opportunity for our own needs to be cared for in the same way. No one wants to be bothered by caring for someone else unnecessarily. It is unhealthy to do so. We also need to consider if we are avoiding the proper care of others by claiming to be bothered. If we do not care for others, we remove the opportunity to produce benefits that can be shared and for our needs to be satisfied.

MAKING GOOD DECISIONS

MODULE 2: LESSON 1

"A GOOD MAN OUT OF THE GOOD TREASURE OF HIS HEART BRINGS FORTH GOOD…"

The Book of Luke 6:45

It can often seem that while we believe we are good people, we find ourselves surrounded by difficulties interacting with others. It is not possible to control the choices other people make. Before we decide others are at fault we must examine our own decisions. It is not enough for a decision to benefit us. We must consider how our decisions affect others.

"HAPPINESS COMES WHEN YOUR WORK AND WORDS ARE OF BENEFIT TO OTHERS" -BUDDHA

Whether or not we agree with the ideas, philosophies or religious beliefs of others, we must accept their existence as a benefit to others in order to be truthful with ourselves. The common teachings of goodness found in beliefs around the word reinforces the common truth of these teachings in each individual belief system. By seeing the need to address these issues in each belief, we can see common needs within our different ideas.

Because a young adult attends church with their parents does not mean they necessarily believe in their parents religious beliefs. Because a particular faith may be judged harshly by opinion does not mean it is without value. Regardless of a student's religious beliefs or lack of religious beliefs, attention needs to be drawn to the role of religion, science and philosophy throughout history. Regardless of affiliation, our beliefs help us understand the elements of living that exist beyond the events we experience. Regardless of professions of faith, each belief system that exists attempts to give wisdom and understanding of how to attain the benefits we all desire beyond what we physically experience.

In today's world many things are identified as "good" and it has become necessary to define the term. What is considered good by one person often offends someone else. This is demonstrated in almost every war and election that occurs around the world. One person has an idea of how things should be, what is "good", gains the support of others in promoting that idea. These people as a group then identify anything that does not immediately reflect their idea as "bad" and we watch conflicts, protests, violence and war on the nightly news.

DEFINITIONS:

GOOD (gud): The opposite of bad; conductive, in general, to any useful end or purpose; serviceable; advantageous; beneficial…possessing desirable or valuable physical or moral qualities…precious; kind; humane; merciful or friendly….; real; actual…more than a little…full or complete….honorable.

PRINCIPLE BEHIND SCRIPTURE:

Throughout history it has become apparent to people throughout the world that the conflicts which occur between groups and nations originate within the hearts and understanding of individuals. All religions and philosophies of understanding identify a selfish desire that exists within all of us as the source of all conflict. The desire to think only of ourselves and a misunderstanding of how we depend on each other for a healthy existence is most commonly addressed in Religion, philosophy and certain sciences by reflecting on demonstrating goodness towards others.

HOW THIS APPLIES TO MAKING GOOD DECISIONS:

Webster's definition of goodness as cited extends 1/3 of the page it was written on and without fully examining the definition, the word can be misunderstood. Every word used in the beginning of the definition can be applied solely to how we treat ourselves and thereby expect others to treat themselves. Without consideration for the differences between different people, we can easily assume that goodness between people is the automatic result of people being good to themselves. This is a common notion in modern society that allows us to place responsibility for disagreements on others without examining our own responsibility in a situation. However, as the definition begins to state "mercy; friendliness…; real; actual" we should understand that for goodness to be "full or complete" and "honorable" goodness requires acknowledgement of things that exist beyond our ideas and ourselves. Our decisions must be good whether or not we agree with others.

MAKING GOOD DECISIONS

MODULE 2: LESSON 1

MAKING DECISIONS THAT BENEFIT OUR LIVES.

We have the ability to produce benefits in all areas of our lives by developing the ability to make good decisions. Many of the decisions we make as adults involve money. Many of our day to day decisions seem completely unrelated to money. Some decisions are simply made possible by the reward of going to work. Other decisions effect more than just what we can afford to buy. Ultimately, the daily decisions we make effect whether or not we have the most important benefits of peace and security for ourselves and others.

WHY DO WE STRUGLLE WITH MAKING GOOD DECISIONS?

Identifying good decisions is something many adults struggle with but it is not difficult. We are faced with the opportunity to make decisions every day**. We are given the opportunity to decide what we are doing in that moment in each moment of the day.** Each day we make a decision to get out of bed. We may make a decision to not get out of bed. We might decide to eat breakfast. We may decide to skip breakfast in order to get somewhere else.

Example 1:

Monday night, Billy chose to watch sport highlights until 1230 am. Tuesday morning Billy hit the snooze button to get up for work at 530am. Billy needs to be at work by 7am so he skipped breakfast because he hit the snooze button. At work, Billy found himself speaking with his supervisor to explain why he took a 20 minute break to eat a snack bar at 830am.

A difficulty that many of us face is not being able to see beyond our immediate circumstances in order to identify the right decision we should make in the moment. What we choose to focus our attention on creates our realities. Billy's morning is a simple example of small decisions we make for ourselves as adults. Without any exaggeration, the small decisions we make as adults can produce larger issues we must deal with later. In the moment we make a decision it may seem completely unrelated to our finances but the decision may later impact our abilities to earn money or have what we need. Billy did not sleep in because the sports highlights were particularly exciting. Billy slept in because he felt tired. That feeling of being tired motivated him to sleep in and skip breakfast. Sleeping in for 15 minutes did not cause Billy to feel more rested and skipping breakfast added the feeling of being hungry. Billy entered work feeling hungry and tired. Feeling hungry and tired, Billy took a twenty minute break after being at work for an hour and a half. The decision to eat a snack bar did not completely satisfy his hunger when his boss spoke with him. After speaking with his supervisor Billy is now tired, hungry and concerned about issues at work. Eventually, Billy has created a reality entirely focused on his feelings and how to resolve them. Our decisions create the circumstances of our lives and our feelings become attached to the experiences we have within the circumstances we create.

Having established the principle that making good decisions must include consideration for our physical surroundings as well as the people we interact with it needs to be understood that most of our daily decisions involve how we function within our physical world. The awareness we keep about others and the world in general should be reflected in the decisions we make managing our individual responsibilities each day.

NOTES: **PERSONAL EXPERIENCES**

____

____

____

____

____

____

____

____

____

____

____

____

____

____

____

____

____

____

____

____

____

____

____

____

____

____

EXAMPLE 1 QUESTIONS:

1. Do you think Billy is a responsible person? Why?_____
____
____
____
____

2. Do you think the supervisor was unreasonable? Why?_
____
____
____

CRITICAL THINKING:

In a few words, explain how you think Billy's day would have been different if he had gone to bed earlier.___________
____
____

In a few words, explain what else Billy might be able to do if he were to set himself a regular bed time each night.____
____
____

GOOD DECISIONS DEPEND ON OUR ABILITY TO SEE BEYOND OURSELVES.

Simple decisions become involved with more important issues and we must manage our feelings by choosing the decisions we make as adults. We can look at the example of Billy and consider it an issue of common sense but within the decisions we make we can each identify where we have robbed ourselves of peace and security. Within each moment of Billy's morning, he attempted to resolve a feeling his decisions had created. As long as Billy was alone, focusing on his feelings without resolving them had very little effect on anything else. Billy was not at peace or secure in his feelings but he felt secure in his ability to deal with being tired and hungry. Billy's focus on his feelings continued as the motivation for his decisions while interacting with others and his decisions effected more than just himself. The reality of life is that even if we live alone, we interact with others. While in our homes we must make decisions to resolve our needs. How we choose to do so impacts the people we meet. We need to be aware of our decisions because we interact with others. **Focusing on how we feel keeps us from seeing the realities of the world around us.** Our decisions will create conflict with something or someone else if we cannot see the realities beyond our feelings.

There are no right or wrong answers to example 1 questions. The student's answers will allow the instructor to asses:

1. General intelligence of the student.
   a. The example is simple and requires only the student's opinion as an answer.
   b. How well the student can look beyond the event in the example to assess the roles responsibilities and proper respect toward others.
   c. How willing or able the student is to relate themselves to the possible feelings of others.
2. How well the subject material is being related.

SUGGESTED ACTIVITY:

Have the student read the paragraph below the answer and explain how their answers relate to what is said.

If the student's answers do not relate: Ask if the student can explain how someone with different experiences than theirs might relate to what is written in the paragraph.

MATURE CONSIDERATION:

Even as youth we are challenged by needing to adjust our decisions in order to meet our responsibilities and this only increases as we grow older. Getting to school on time becomes getting to work and eventually we need to live on our own or with others we must be responsible for. Decisions that appear to affect no one but ourselves often effect everyone around us. As adults it is our responsibility to examine our perspectives regularly and change them when necessary.

MAKING GOOD DECISIONS

MODULE 2: LESSON 2

CHANGING OUR PERSPECTIVES

We cannot change the realities of the circumstances we live in for each decision we make. Often we need to change our perspectives in order to see the right decision we must make. The realities of the need to work and interacting with others are not going to change. We must find a way to change our perspectives in order to make decisions within these realities. Each person creates their realities in the same way. This can often cause obstacles to seeing things clearly. Because we each make our own decisions, it is not possible for us to remove an obstacle to someone else agreeing with the circumstances and decisions we recognize. Likewise, it is not possible for others remove the obstacles that sometimes keep us from identifying a good decision. **We must each be willing to change our perspectives and make decisions to remove obstacles from our own view of each circumstance**.

Most often when something cannot be seen it is because something exists between ourselves and what we are trying to see. In many cases we can remove an object that blocks our vision. In other circumstances the object may be a fixed reality that requires us to change our position and perspective. As adults we deal with both.

We must first identify the obstacles we can remove from our perspectives in order for us to see the realities of any situation. Some circumstances may cause us to feel that we are required to examine everything we believe we know. Doing so would only cause confusion and many people refuse to change their perspectives on anything because of this confusion. Certain realities do not need to be questioned and a world full of people will not change positions so we can see how to make decisions for our lives. **The individual ability of each person to make their own decisions is why some people make good decisions and others do not.**

NOTES: **PERSONAL EXPERIENCES**

____

____

____

____

____

____

____

____

____

____

____

____

____

The first paragraph CHANGING OUR PERSPECTIVES is intended to pick up where Lesson 1 ended. Introducing the subject of individual perspectives creating personal realities and discussing how individual realities interact with each other and the realities of the world around us.

QUESTIONS:

3. Is there an experience you can remember when you felt convinced of being right but discovered you were wrong?
4. Is there an experience you can remember when you were uncertain of what the right decision to make?

OPPORTTUNITY FOR DISCUSSION:

As people we may be convinced that we are right in our opinions and ideas but not understand the circumstances as well as we think we do. We may make a decision without considering anything other than what we think is right and find we have offended someone or lost an opportunity to do something in a way we did not intend. Because we are not all knowing we can be faced with situations involving others or in circumstances where we are not certain of a right decision to make. In these situations it is helpful to stop and consider our values and responsibilities as well as those of others compared to the circumstances in order to make a good decision.

MAKING GOOD DECISIONS

MODULE 2: LESSON 2

WHEN ARE WE RESPONSIBLE FOR MAKING A DECISION?

We must first identify what exists as a removable obstacle for ourselves if we hope to gain a better perspective in any circumstance. We are given an opportunity to identify possible obstacles we have the ability to remove when we are faced with a decision that creates conflict within ourselves. **We must be able to identify where conflict exists in order to make good decisions.**

The existence of conflict within a situation does not mean there is an obstacle we can remove. If we identify a conflict between ourselves and another person, place or thing we can only identify what we can change by knowing what we can control. We may be able to argue our opinion to a point of agreement between ourselves and someone else but whether or not the conflict is replaced with a peaceful and secure reality depends on each person's decisions. Most often, the only thing an argument creates is the need to apologize. If we have conflict entering a door that is locked we might knock but beating on the door is not likely to unlock it. Likewise kicking our car and yelling is not going to change a flat tire. **Because each person makes their own decisions and the physical realities of what things are will not change; we can only control the decisions we make.** We can only move what we can control. Whether or not we can change the existence of conflict by our own decisions determines what we can change.

In most conflicts there exists something each individual can do to replace it with Peace and Security. If we are in a conflict, we must ask ourselves how we contribute to the conflict. If we park our car in the middle of a parking lot because we are waiting for someone: we may be approached by someone who cannot move around our car when they want to leave. We have simply placed ourselves and our desire for convenience in someone else's way. Whether or not they are upset does not change our ability to remove the obstacle we have created. We can choose to use a parking space if we wish to avoid the possibility of being approached in this manner. We must address things that cause us daily conflict in the same way. If we know we have to be at work by a certain time; we can choose to set ourselves a schedule to ensure we get enough sleep, eat breakfast and not carry ourselves to work tired or hungry. Whether or not our supervisor is a reasonable person, we have removed our part in creating a conflict. We remove the conflict of our feelings from effecting ourselves and others in a negative way by making a responsible decision to manage time. In each of these examples the decisions made do not depend on changing the realities of what things are or attempting to influence others. Our decisions have not placed us in a position to be victimized by unreasonable people, unnecessarily concerned with the wellbeing of others or victimized by the results of our own decisions. **Peace and Security are produced for ourselves and others by making responsible decisions to care for ourselves.** When we are able to identify how we can replace conflict with peace and security without the need to change others or the realities of life: we have identified a good decision we are responsible to make.

As individuals, what we can control is limited to the, thoughts, ideas, decisions and actions we make. At school or work we may be able to set tasks, establish goals and create new physical realities within the dynamic of a collective group. In our families the same possibility exists as well. However, there is little we can do to change the basic realities of the world we live in and absolutely nothing we can do to change the people around us without their consent. We can only truly control our own choices and those choices create the realities we live in on a daily basis.

OPPORTUNITY FOR DISCUSSION:

It is very true that we will occasionally encounter situations where conflict arises or exists without our involvement and in these situations we can choose to participate in conflict or remove ourselves from it. However, most conflicts we encounter on a daily basis involve decisions we have or need to make. In most situations where conflict exists each person has in some way contributed to the conflict. By examining our choices we can discover better decisions or the reality that there is nothing we can do to remove the conflict. In either case, we remove the conflict from our own lives by understanding the choices we can make.

MAKING GOOD DECISIONS STARTS AT HOME.

Our greatest benefits of Peace and Security are also needs that exist within the lives of each individual. Much philosophical debate could be given to state that Love exists in this same manner as both a benefit of life and a need we each have. For the sake of simplicity, we can say that Love does not grow where peace and security do not exist. With that understanding we can examine every decision we make and the benefit we desire from making those decisions. If we purchase a home or piece of furniture, it is out of a desire for that decision to provide us comfort. Our sense of comfort is an extension of our desire for Peace and Security. It is possible to argue that no other benefits in life also exist as true needs.

Conflict is created for us in any situation that removes our Peace and Security. The best way to replace conflict with peace and security is to remove the possibility of conflict in any circumstance we can.The place we are most responsible for making decisions is within our homes . The decisions we make at home create the circumstances and realities we face whenever we are home. If we do not pay our rent or mortgage, we will not have a home to live in. If we do not pay our utilities, we will not have light to see or hot water to clean with. These are basic realities we cannot change. However, simply making the decisions required by life's realities does not provide us with both peace and security. We may have the security of knowing food is in the refrigerator and the rent is payed while still living with conflict.

EXAMPLE 2:

Johnny goes to work and pays his bills. Each day Johnny eats breakfast, goes to work, comes home from work and calls Sally before sitting down to watch the television. On Mondays and Tuesdays Johnny usually cooks himself an easy meal before going to bed. On Wednesdays Johnny goes to Church and meets friends for dinner afterward. On Thursdays, Johnny usually grabs breakfast on the way to work and fast food for dinner on the way home. When Fridays arrive, Johnny finds he is glad to have made it through the week even though he is exhausted. Unfortunately, on Saturdays Johnny is realizing that Sally usually has other plans for when he wants to hang out. Johnny spends every Saturday washing the dishes from the week, catching up on laundry before watching a movie and ordering a pizza. On Sunday Johnny goes to morning church service, watches the game on TV and folds half of the laundry he washed the day before. Most of his clothes are too small and Johnny needs to buy new ones. Johnny does not understand why Sally always seems busy. This week he did not get the promotion he had expected and as he approaches the age of 23 he reflects on how he never thought he would feel this old. As this thought crosses Johnny's mind, he begins to sneeze and realizes he has caught the cold he has had this time each year for the last 4 years. Sunday night Johnny develops a fever and calls in sick for work on Monday.

Any time we feel conflict, the natural human reaction is to re-create the same situations that previously existed when we felt Peace and Security. As children when we encountered conflict we:

Argued: The result of being emotionally overwhelmed, unable to communicate and/or understand the circumstances. (Ages 2-?)

Asked someone else to resolve the conflict: The result of being emotionally overwhelmed, unable to communicate and/or understand the circumstances. (Ages 2-?)

Some adults never mature beyond this.

Developing maturity requires us to recognize conflict as an opportunity to pause, ask ourselves what we desire, if our desires are possible to acquire within the realities of the circumstances and if our choices are actually accomplishing what we desire. This is part of developing a mature perspective on life.

We should not base the reason for our decisions in what we believe other people want or expect but we must consider what is commonly appreciated by most people. Are our decisions placing undue responsibility on others or creating an environment around us that conflicts with the healthy needs of others? These are questions it is healthy to consider when examining our decisions.

MAKING GOOD DECISIONS

MODULE 2: LESSON 2

EXAMPLE 2 QUESTIONS:

1. Does Johnny seem like a good person? Why?________
2. Does Johnny seem like a responsible person? Why?____
3. Does Johnny eat healthy food? How do you know?_____
4. Does Johnny Exercise? How do you know? __________
5. Other than doing laundry and dishes, does Johnny clean his house regularly? How do you know?_____________
6. Do you think Johnny is healthy? Why?______________
7. Do you think Johnny is Happy?____________________

CRITICAL THINKING:

In a few words, explain if you think Johnny plans when he will do his laundry, if he does it when he feels he can or both? _______

In a few words, explain what you think Johnny and his clothes might look like when he goes to work and church.____________

In a few words, explain why you think Sally might not want to hang out with Johnny on Saturdays anymore._______________

Having established a mature understanding that:

Good decisions benefit ourselves and others

Good decisions require consideration for the differences between ourselves and others while recognizing our common needs.

Our individual decisions may appear to effect only ourselves but most often effect everyone around us no matter how simple the decision may be.

When we are faced with conflict it is an opportunity to examine our own choices and make decisions to remove resolve the conflict or remove ourselves from it.

We need to consider the real life effects of our decisions when examining how we view our own decisions and the decisions of others.

SUGGESTED ACTIVITY:

Ask the student to place themselves in the role of the character Sally understanding that Johnny and Sally were high school sweethearts. Ask the student if there is anything Sally can do to improve Johnny's life without being responsible for things Johnny needs to do for himself.

Actually making decisions that provide ourselves and others with respect for our common individual defines whether or not our decisions can be considered GOOD MATURE ADULT DECISIONS.

MAKING GOOD DECISIONS

MODULE 2: LESSON 2

TOPIC SUMMARY

There is no one else who will be able to manage our responsibilities for us as adults. In each of the examples of Billy and Johnny, their decisions at home had effects on how they felt and how they interacted with the people around them. **Whether or not our decisions appear responsible we must be aware of the realities they create in our lives.** When we become independent adults, our parents are not present to clean our homes, cook our meals, or make sure that we are healthy. Our co-workers and friends will not be concerned with whether or not we can do these things for ourselves as adults. We are responsible to make our own decisions as individuals. We must be able to identify good decisions for ourselves as adults. **Each person has a need for Peace and Security.** Peace and Security are also benefits we create for ourselves by making good decisions. If the decisions we make create conflicts, we must be able to identify how we can remove conflict by making better decisions. **In order to see where conflicts are created we must be able to see beyond our feelings and perspectives in order to see circumstances as they truly are.** We will be able to produce benefits and rewards that bring peace and security to our lives while considering the same desires and needs of others if we can identify good decisions.

TOPIC ASSIGNMENT:

While our decisions can create obvious conflicts between ourselves and others they can also create conflicts for ourselves which are not as obvious to us. Write 3-4 paragraphs (4-5 sentences each) Based on all your answers within this chapter. Describe the conflicts you think exist in Johnny's life and decisions he could make to remove those conflicts. Try to find similarities between Billy and Johnny's conflicts that may help you find good decisions Johnny can make.

____
____
____
____
____
____
____
____
____
____
____
____
____

The Topic Summary is a brief description of why we must make responsible decisions to avoid conflict, how we can identify the need to make different decisions by identifying where conflict exists and the benefits produced by making good decisions.

<u>There are no correct answers to the topic assignment.</u>

The Topic Assignment allows the instructor to gain a perspective of the students, thoughts feelings and opinions in order to establish a foundation for discussing the final portion of the Training Module.

Instructions for "BOLD REALITIES" section:

Bold Realities for Discussion are portions of the text which appear in **Bold Type** within the Training Module. It is suggested that the discussion of these principles be conducted in an informal manner. Discussing this portion casually reinforces the understanding of the subject material within the mind of the student. This forum allows that understanding to be freely expressed without the requirement of structured questions, answers or written assignments.

BOLD REALITIES

FOR DISCUSSION

By making good decisions we can satisfy our greatest needs in life. We have the ability to produce benefits in all areas of our lives by developing the ability to make good decisions. In each moment of the day we are given the opportunity to decide what we are doing in that moment.

What we choose to focus our attention on creates our realities. Our decisions create the circumstances of our lives and our feelings become attached to the experiences we have within the circumstances we create. Focusing on how we feel keeps us from seeing the realities of the world around us. We must each be willing to change our perspectives and make decisions to remove obstacles from our own view of each circumstance.

The individual ability of each person to make their own decisions is why some people make good decisions and others do not. In order to make good decisions we must be able to identify where conflict exists. Because each person makes their own decisions and the physical realities of what things are will not change; we can only control the decisions we make.

Peace and Security are produced for ourselves and others by making responsible decisions to care for ourselves. Conflict is created for us in any situation that removes our Peace and Security. Whether or not our decisions appear responsible we must be aware of the realities they create in our lives. Each person has a need for Peace and Security.

In order to see where conflicts are created we must be able to see beyond our feelings and perspectives in order to see circumstances as they truly are.

RESULTS & CONSEQUENCES

THE MOTIVATIONS BEHIND OUR CHOICES

It is a simple fact that we make decisions based on the expected results or consequences of our actions. However, not all of our decisions truly benefit us. **If our goal in life is to be happy, fulfilled and successful we need to examine the reasons we make choices.** By examining the results of our actions we can determine whether or not our choices are based in a motivation that benefits us or if we are motivated by something that brings us undesirable consequences.

NOTES: **PERSONAL EXPERIENCES**

____

____

____

____

____

The picture is intended to be discussed with the student (Following reading of the introductory paragraph and the sections titled "Why do we form habits?", " How can habits create conflicts?","How do we identify habits that need to change?" & "How do we change a habit?").

Each star designates an element of the picture to be discussed.

Questions to ask the student:

12. Does the girl seem to be happy?
13. Does there seem to be a minor mess that needs cleaning?
14. Is it possible the child is missing her front teeth from regularly being given sugary treats?

The results of our decisions may produce more than what we initially consider as results and consequences. The intended results of our decisions usually have some benefit for ourselves and others. When we discover a decision that produces these benefits we are likely to repeat making that decision regardless of minor inconveniences it may cause us. Ultimately these decisions which when repeated become habits we rely on and can cause consequences for ourselves and others which we may not consider.

RESULTS AND CONSEQUENCES

MODULE 3: LESSON 1

THE MOTIVATIONS BEHIND OUR CHOICES

Why do we form Habits?

Habits form in order to complete tasks or deal with circumstances we encounter. The motivation to repeat an action or behavior is found in the reward we identify for ourselves by doing a task or responding to a circumstance in a particular way. The identified reward provides us some level of comfort and we repeat a decision to get that reward until repetition becomes a habit. In most cases a habit forms for the benefit of making a task or circumstance less difficult for ourselves. The result of creating a habit is our individual ability to function with difficulty in any given circumstance.

How can Habits create conflict?

As we develop into maturity we learn that our decisions have consequences for ourselves and others. Habits we have formed are based in our motivations to care and protect ourselves but can conflict with the habits of others. As we reach an age when others expect and depend on us to care for more than just ourselves, we discover many of the habits we have formed cause difficulty for those around us. The consequence of maintaining these habits is continuing conflict between ourselves and others.

How do we identify the Habits that need to change?

Not all habits need to change. Good Habits combined to form daily routines benefit ourselves and those around us. In identifying bad habits the simplest approach is to identify the choices we make that provide no benefit to others and produce rewards only for ourselves. In each situation that creates conflict we must simply ask ourselves if what we are doing has any benefit for the people around us. If the answer is no, we need to accept that our bad habit needs to change.

How do we change a habit?

Trying to repeat a new behavior in order to replace an old one often fails because the motivation that created the habit is never identified. Many of our bad habits will have a shared motivation. To change a bad habit we must be able to recognize a new motivation for repeating a new behavior. We must appreciate the result of doing something new more than we appreciate our reason for doing what is familiar.

NOTES: **PERSONAL EXPERIENCES**

____

____

Time should be allotted for cooperative reading of the subject material. Engaging the student actively reading in a shared environment requires the student to participate vocally and actively listen.

As individuals we form habits to make our lives and addressing regular responsibilities easier. Because we are individuals with personally unique experiences and talents, we do not often consider how our habits may cause difficulty for others who interact with and depend on us.

Many of the habits we form do not fully address how something should or could be done while we are young and cared for by others. As adults we may find that our habits may cause conflict. We are responsible to address that conflict by changing our habits or repeatedly dealing with the difficulties they create.

QUESTIONS:

1. Can you identify something you do that repeatedly causes arguments with someone else?
2. Can you identify why you do this?
3. Is doing this worth the arguing it creates?

If we can identify the habits which cause difficulty for ourselves and others simply trying to do something different often fails unless we identify the motivation we have for doing something a certain way.

RESULTS AND CONSEQUENCES

MODULE 3: LESSON 1

"GOOD HABITS FORMED AT YOUTH MAKE ALL THE DIFFERENCE".

-Aristotle

The habits we identify in ourselves and others are actions that reflect how we think. Habits form based on our thoughts and feelings about how we can feel good about ourselves while accomplishing things we must do. Whenever we are faced with a new task we often think of how we have dealt with challenges in the past. As we mature between childhood and adulthood we must consider if our reasons for how and why we do things must change.

Attention needs to be drawn to the role of religion, science and philosophy throughout history. Regardless of professions of faith, each belief system that exists attempts to give wisdom and understanding of how to attain the type of life we all desire through the choices we make.

PRINCIPLE BEHIND QUOTE:

Throughout history it has become apparent to people throughout the world that the conflicts which occur between groups and nations originate within the hearts and understanding of individuals. All belief systems place great importance on the actions we take matching a moral standard of thought we should all be conscious of in our daily lives.

HOW THIS APPLIES TO MAKING RESULTS AND CONSEQUENCES:

Aristotle was a student and teacher of Platonic philosophy at a time in history when great thought was being given to understanding ourselves, our place within the world and how we interact with the world around us. Within Platonic philosophies are found the principles of questioning what we would not normally question in order to discover why and how we do things which Socrates taught and Plato is attributed with recording. Much thought and writing was given by both Plato and Aristotle to develop an understanding of how we exist in our world as physical, intellectual and spiritual beings. These were some of the earliest and still considered some of the most profound studies and observations into human nature that have contributed to much of what we consider true about human existence today. Within these philosophical teachings it is clearly understood that in order to realize our greatest human potential it is the responsibility of the individual person to understand and practice these things for themselves.

In this quote Aristotle is stating that habits formed at a young age make all the difference in what results or consequences a person may face as they live their lives interacting with the world around them.

NOTES: **PERSONAL EXPERIENCES**

____
____
____
____
____
____
____
____

HOW DO OUR HABITS EFFECT US?

Most habits we form have some benefit for us but are not formed with consideration of how they might effect those around us. We may form the habit of brushing our teeth regularly after breakfast but never floss or use mouth wash. Perhaps flossing feels too awkward or mouthwash is something we were never given to use. We may form the habit of taking a shower every other day and leaving the towel on the floor. Perhaps, when we were seven our mother told us we did not need to shower every day and we never noticed the towel was always hung up or replaced when we got home from school. **As children things may never have seemed to be an issue but as we get older things change.** Without changing our habits as we mature, we will find people asking if we have brushed our teeth, flatly stating our breath smells bad, our body smells bad and more than likely having our parents tell us we need to put our dirty towels in the laundry.

Our responsibilities change with our physical growth and abilities as we mature. For example, the spaces between our teeth grow larger and trap pieces of food between them that brushing cannot remove. The pieces of food stuck between our teeth begin to decay and cause our gums to become infected. If we do not floss our teeth and rinse using mouthwash, we form a condition known as Halitosis that can cause our breath to smell like rotting food from several feet away. Our bodies also begin to sweat, releasing toxins and oils through our skin. The hormones produced by our body as we grow older increase the amount of toxins that are combined with oils in our skin as we sweat. If we do not shower every day, these oils and toxins collect dirt on our bodies and in our hair which also cause us to smell from several feet away. People do not like to sit next to something or someone that smells. Our parents are not likely to enjoy touching the towel we use every two days. The time of being a child who is cute with some dirt on their face has ended. We now realize the smell we produce by maintaining our childhood habits negatively effects the people around us and causes us embarrassment. We are also large enough and aware enough for the laundry room not to be a place we will accidentally poison ourselves. Because we are now of a physical size and ability to care for ourselves, people expect us to take responsibility for our own care in a way that is not offensive to others and does not cause ourselves embarrassment.

In many cases our habits create difficulties we become comfortable with and are not apparent to us. The previous examples discussed are something most people can relate a common experience with because we all have similar experiences connected to our physical development. However, if someone has never been told their breath stinks or to pick up the towel they leave on the ground; they may choose to ignore how someone else covers their nose or not realize how they leave messes for others to clean up as they become older. Our habits become things we rely on that give us confidence we have done things properly, know how to care for ourselves and do not need to concern ourselves with changing. Unfortunately, having a comfortable sense of confidence does not mean we know how to care for ourselves.

Having established the principles that:

1. Habits are formed in order to make our lives easier.
2. Our habits often effect everyone around us.
3. It is each individuals responsibility to be aware of how we interact with others.

Our responsibilities change and our habits may not serve a purpose as well as they once did as we mature.

As adults, we must be aware of the possibility that we are unaware of how our habits affect others.

TYPES OF DIFFICULTY & CONFLICT:

Embarrassment
Arguments
Repeated comments by others
Things that interfere with our abilities to do other things.

OPPORTUNITY FOR DISCUSSION:

When we feel embarrassment or hear repeated comments by others which can lead to arguments; we can feel personally judged before considering anything else.

RESULTS AND CONSEQUENCES

MODULE 3: LESSON 1

EXAMPLE 1:

Sally always learned things quickly. From a young age Sally enjoyed helping her parents. Learning things did not seem like work to Sally because every time she learned how to do something on her own she was given the chance to do something she liked. The summer between Junior High and High School she got a bowl of ice cream after washing the dishes every weekend evening. That same summer, her dad took her to see her favorite movie when she learned to completely do her own laundry. Sally knew that when she learned to do something she would get something she enjoyed for learning it.

When Sally started high school things changed. Sally didn't know why things seemed harder to learn but they were. Sally didn't think her classes were extremely difficult and her grades were good but she felt frustrated. To Sally, it seemed like all of her time was spent either going to school, washing her laundry, doing her homework or washing the dishes. Sally's dad offered her ice cream on the weekends but she didn't want it anymore. She was not fat but Sally noticed she was not as thin as some of the other girls at school.

During Winter Break, Sally talked to her parents about how frustrated she felt. Her mom and dad listened patiently. Before they said anything Sally eagerly showed them her Report Card proudly stating "all A's and 2 B's". Her parents quietly looked at each other smiling before responding. Both of Sally's parents told her that they were very proud of her grades and they understood her frustration. Sally was a little disappointed when her mother said, "Most often, life's greatest reward for doing well is the confidence we get from knowing how hard we have worked". Sally and her parents talked a few more times before she went back to school. Hearing about how life works as an adult is not what she expected or wanted to hear. However, when the first day of the new semester started, Sally was no longer frustrated. Throughout the rest of the year Sally's friends came over to visit with her family on the weekends and help each other with homework. They even went to the movies a couple times. By the end of the school year, Sally felt like Christmas had just ended.

NOTES: PERSONAL EXPERIENCES________________

____
____
____
____
____
____
____
____

During our youth we form our abilities to deal with change but may not be aware of why we become frustrated or what we actually desire from life as we go through change. In this example Sally faces that exact circumstance as she navigates maturing from childhood to youth with the same responsibilities she has always accepted and learning to adjust to changing realities.

Two perspectives of how this transition can be viewed are presented in how Sally approaches her situation and in how Sally's parents respond. The perspective of a child learning as they mature and the perspective of an understanding adult who has already experienced these difficulties.

OPPORTUNITY FOR DISCUSSION:

Many people mature to adulthood without developing an understanding that maturity does not come with age. Many adults often behave no differently than when they were teenagers. When we look at the idea of the type of life we would like to live as adults, we often do not consider the maturity it will require to have a larger life filled with greater responsibilities and lasting relationships. Whether or not we wish or plan to have children we become responsible for the well-being of others in all types of adult relationships. It is healthy to consider how much understanding we would like to give the people we care for and begin applying the type of thinking it requires. Like anything else, mature thinking takes practice in order to apply. When we choose to begin practicing anything determines how soon it will become a habit in our lives.

QUESTION:

Would you rather be the person who responds without understanding or the person who is relied on to understand?

RESULTS AND CONSEQUENCES

MODULE 3: LESSON 1

EXAMPLE 1 QUESTIONS:

1. What do you think was Sally's motivation for learning new things? Why?

2. Why do you think Sally felt frustrated?

3. Why do you think Sally was eager to show her parents her report card?

4. Do you think the things Sally enjoyed were changing? Explain How?

CRITICAL THINKING

1. In a few words explain why you think Sally was disappointed by what her parents told her?

2. In a few words explain why you think Sally did not get frustrated during the rest of the year if her schoolwork and chores did not change.

There are no right or wrong answers to example 1 questions.

SUGGESTED ACTIVITY:

Discuss the students answers within the context of Example 1 opportunity for discussion.

NOTES:

RESULTS AND CONSEQUENCES

MODULE 3: LESSON 2

WE ALL SHARE COMMON MOTIVATIONS FOR CREATING HABITS.

From an early age, the greatest challenge we have to face is how to function within the world around us. **As we learn to do things, the decisions that give us the ability to function create a sense of accomplishment we define as success.** When we feel we have achieved success we then feel secure that we have learned to function.

Whether motivated by time, difficulty, necessity or enjoyment we develop ways of learning and doing things at the same time. When we are little children we have the luxury of learning to feed ourselves, go to the bathroom on our own and various other functions by doing one task at a time. However, as we grow older our world becomes larger as more activities become a part of our lives. This requires us to learn new tasks at the same time. Most of us never really master any particular task as a child. This is due to the fact we begin learning something we need to do before we have truly finished learning to do something else. Things such as brushing our teeth, dressing ourselves and eating breakfast regularly become part of learning how to arrive somewhere on time. **Within this process we learn that not everything can be done exactly how we would like every time we do it.** Because we were children, our lives and schedules were not within our control. If we felt rushed or had difficulty as children most often do, we did not find enjoyment in taking the time to do things properly. As learning to do things became chores, our focus as children was in doing what we had to so we could do the things we enjoyed. Cleaning our rooms was less important than playing a game, playing with friends or anything we did not feel was work. Out of the necessity to meet increasing responsibilities, we develop habits of learning that minimize the difficulties of trying to do multiple things within a limited amount of time.

As we grow older the habits we have do not always work well for ourselves or others. Because we all have different homes in which we were raised, we all have differing ideas of what we need to be responsible in doing. Because we all have similar basic needs and differing ideas of responsibilities, the habits we feel secure our ability to function may not be as well developed as the habits of another person. For each individual, the result of having developed habits is the sense of security each person feels they have within their ability to function. Likewise for each individual, the consequence of having developed habits is that our sense of security becomes challenged when our habits do not reflect the habits of others.

Having established the principles that:

4. Habits are formed in order to make our lives easier.
5. Our habits often effect everyone around us.
6. It is each individual's responsibility to be aware of how we interact with others.
7. Personal conflicts are opportunities to question what we do rather than feel judged by others.
8. As we mature, our habits should adjust to reflect greater responsibility and care for those we love.

It is important to understand that each person develops habits in the same general way based in their individual experiences. Beyond simply making things easier for ourselves, we also develop habits in order to be able to multitask. In most cases, a habitual method of getting things done is motivated by the desire to finish several tasks we do not like so we can have time to do something we enjoy. In doing so tasks are not necessarily completed or fully addressed as they might be by someone else who learned to do the same thing under different circumstances.

QUESTIONS:

1. Have you ever argued about how to do something?
2. Is it more important to feel right or do something correctly?

RESULTS AND CONSEQUENCES

MODULE 3: LESSON 2

EXAMPLE 2:

Johnny never really thought much about chores. Johnny understood he needed to do things because if he didn't his parents would get upset, he would get grounded and lose something he enjoyed. When Johnny went to church as a kid, his hair was neatly combed and he made sure he tied his shoes with a double not. The rest of the week, Johnny's mom would threaten to cut the hair off his head and the laces off his shoes if he didn't fix them both.

Johnny had always been fast and when he started High School he earned a place on the Junior Varsity Track Team. Johnny liked talking to Sally, whose first class after lunch was on the opposite side of the school from his. Johnny would walk Sally to class and sprint across the campus. Johnny was fast but he was also late to class on a regular basis. Johnny found himself in detention more than once. Johnny didn't worry about it much because he knew he could talk to Sally on the phone after school so he wouldn't be late. Johnny started making it to class on time and called Sally every day after track practice.

A few weeks later the coach told Johnny that he would not be able to run with the team. Going to detention and not completing homework had caused Johnny to be placed on Academic Probation until his grades improved.

EXAMPLE 2 QUESTIONS:

1. Do you think Johnny is responsible or tries to avoid getting in trouble? Why?______________________________
____
____
2. What do you think is Johnny's motivation for doing things?
____
____
3. If Johnny's habits towards his responsibilities do not change: Do you think Johnny will have other problems? Why?___
____
____
4. If Johnny's grades improve and his habits towards his responsibilities do not change: Do you think he will make the Varsity Track Team? Why?______________________
____
____

We often form a habitual way of doing things that does not take into consideration different levels of responsibility to ourselves and others without realizing it consciously. In this example Johnny addresses his responsibilities to school and his team in the same way he addresses doing chores at home. With greater responsibilities a greater awareness of consequences and how to achieve our desired results needs to be applied if we wish to be considered mature adults. We need to be aware of how we habitually form habits within different areas of our lives that require different levels of responsibility. Beyond this simple example exists a reality that most people never mature beyond their youth. Many adults continue to be unaware of how they form habits within new circumstances as they age.

QUESTIONS:

Revisit Example 2 of Making Good Decisions. Consider Johnny and Sally's relationship after High School.

1. Did Johnny ever change how he felt about doing chores or formed habits?
2. In either example: Is it in any way Sally's <u>responsibility</u> to tell Johnny how he should make decisions?
3. Why would Johnny <u>need</u> someone to address the consequences of his bad habits?
4. Why should we <u>need</u> someone to point out the consequences of our bad habits?

RESULTS AND CONSEQUENCES

MODULE 3: LESSON 2

TOPIC SUMMARY

Ultimately, our habits are directly connected to our identity. **The longer a habit exists the more secure we feel within our capability to do the thing we have formed a habit around.** Eventually, we identify ourselves with how well we can do things or perform based on our abilities. If we have been consistent in forming good habits, the security we have within our identities is not often challenged. However, we may also not recognize the need to change if we are overly confident in ourselves and unaware of our poor habits. **If the motivation behind our decisions benefits only ourselves we will often find ourselves in conflict with others or our ability to do things we want to do.**

TOPIC ASSIGNMENT

Considering what you have read, write a 3-4 paragraphs

(3-5 sentences each) reflecting on one of your own bad habits, the motivation behind it and why it might be good to change. Ask someone you live with if you need help.

___

___

___

___

___

___

___

___

___

___

___

___

___

___

___

___

___

___

___

___

___

___

___

We identify ourselves by our experiences and how well or how poorly we have felt about the results and consequences our experiences have created. Good habits most often create good results and cause us to feel confident in who we are. However, that confidence may also exist because we never question what we feel confident about. As mature adults we must examine the results and consequences of our lives. We should examine our habits with the goal of being the type of person we want to be who is also capable of doing the things we want to do without conflict.

SUGGESTED ACTIVITY:

Discuss with the student the type of values they would like to demonstrate as a person and what personal goals or interests they may have. In this discussion ask the student to examine what habits they may have that conflict with demonstrating those values, achieving those goals or maintaining those interests. Select one or two habits that can reasonably be addressed and set a goal to do something differently in order to create a habit that reflects the desired values, goals and interests.

NOTES: **PERSONAL EXPERIENCES**

___

___

___

___

___

___

___

___

___

___

___

___

___

Instructions for "BOLD REALITIES" section:

Bold Realities for Discussion are portions of the text which appear in **Bold Type** within the Training Module. It is suggested that the discussion of these principles be conducted in an informal manner. Discussing this portion casually reinforces the understanding of the subject material within the mind of the student. This forum allows that understanding to be freely expressed without the requirement of structured questions, answers or written assignments. It is suggested that each be discussed separately and within the context how they are combined.

BOLD REALITIES

FOR DISCUSSION

If our goal in life is to be happy, fulfilled and successful we need to examine the reasons we make choices. Most habits we form have some benefit for us but are not formed with consideration of how they might effect those around us. As children things may never have seemed to be an issue but as we get older things change. In many cases our habits create difficulties we become comfortable with and are not apparent to us.

As we learn to do things, the decisions that give us the ability to function create a sense of accomplishment we define as success. Within this process we learn that not everything can be done exactly how we would like every time we do it.

The longer a habit exists the more secure we feel within our capability to do the thing we have formed a habit around. If the motivation behind our decisions benefits only ourselves we will often find ourselves in conflict with others or being able to do things we want to do.

SELF AWARENESS

WHAT TO DO IN CONFLICT AND ADVERSITY

As we transition from childhood to adulthood, we mature through a stage of life known as youth. What we have been responsible for as children changes. We are faced with new challenges. Our lives expand to include more people, places and things. Our awareness of the differences between ourselves and others cause us to question our ideas while we are learning more about the people and the world around us.

Awareness of ourselves and our desires becomes a central focus of our attention during our youth. We realize many of childhood's rules no longer apply. Many of us feel that if we are expected to be more responsible, we should also be allowed to address our responsibilities in our own way.

During our youth we develop the ideas we use to manage conflict as adults. We want both the independence of adulthood and the free spirited life of childhood. Experiences that oppose our desires for both adulthood and childhood places all of us within the adversity of youth. Our choices within adversity often place us in conflict with others. Our ability to recognize if and when we need to change determines how well we will deal with conflict as adults.

The picture is intended to be discussed with the student (Following reading of the introductory paragraph and the sections titled "We all develop the same way", "Why it sometimes does not work?" & "How do we change what does not work?"). Each star designates an element of the picture to be discussed.

Questions to ask the student:

15. Do you think there was a time when the girl could not reach the sink?
16. From the look on the girls face, does she feel confident in her ability to wash her own hands?
17. Do you see any soap being used in the picture?

We graduate through experiences forgetting the challenges we faced in learning how to do things. Where conflict existed within our ability to accomplish regular activities a sense of self confidence develops. It is often our confidence that blinds us to what we may still need to learn about things we think we know. Many adults reach an age when youth ends and stop thinking about what we may not know. With the challenges of life and work, our personal sense of confidence in doing things becomes something we identify ourselves by in order to face these new challenges. Our general sense of personal confidence can blind us to why we have conflict with the people we care for.

SELF AWARENESS

MODULE 4: LESSON 1

WE ALL DEVELOP THE SAME WAY

As people we graduate through experiences that by success, failure and disappointment teach us to manage difficulty, conflict and pain. A child learns to walk, run and ride a bike by continually falling until they learn. Similarly, as we grow older challenges in forming relationships cause us emotional difficulty, conflict and pain. In youth we develop tools for managing conflict and adversity that we feel protect us from pain, disappointment and failure.

WHY IT SOMETIMES DOES NOT WORK?

As we mature toward adulthood we learn to resist changing what we know works for us. Each individual develops a sense of security in how they have learned to do things. When conflict arises from differences of opinion or ideas, each person involved is actually faced with their sense of security being threatened. This is because how a person thinks, functions and feels in any given circumstance is based in their idea of themselves and who they are. **When a situation challenges our ideas and abilities we feel that our identity as a person is being challenged.**

HOW DO WE CHANGE WHAT DOES NOT WORK?

As human beings each person must recognize a need to change before a change can be made. We all establish comfortable ways we do things in order to make our lives easier. Difficulty and conflict cause us to feel insecure in or capabilities. When we realize that we create our individual realities through the decisions we make, we begin to see how our methods of protecting ourselves often place us in conflict with how others make their decisions. When we understand that it is not possible to make others change, we must then look at how we can resolve our own difficulties. By recognizing what we are responsible for we can gain the perspective necessary to make individual changes and remove ourselves from conflict.

NOTES: **PERSONAL EXPERIENCES**

____

____

____

____

____

____

____

____

____

____

____

____

Time should be allotted for cooperative reading of the subject material. Engaging the student actively reading in a shared environment requires the student to participate vocally and actively listen.

As adults we need to examine where and from what types of experiences our Identity has developed. If we have had success in doing particular things we may believe we have the ability to instruct others but that belief does not take into consideration what others may know or believe they know. If we have experienced failure or lack experience in certain activities we may avoid involvement in those activities and allow others to do things we feel better not doing. However, that preference or avoidance does not take into consideration what we should be responsible for doing and may unfairly require others to do for us.

QUESTIONS:

4. Can you identify something you Do or do not do that repeatedly causes arguments with someone else?
5. Can you identify why you do this?
6. Is doing or not doing this worth the arguing it creates?
7. Do you ever walk away from these arguments feeling at peace with who you are or upset with how others treat you?

SELF AWARENESS

MODULE 4: LESSON 1

THE BEGINNING OF STRIFE IS LIKE RELEASING WATER; THEREFORE STOP CONTENTION BEFORE A QUARREL STARTS

The Book of Proverbs 17:6

When we are confronted with adversity we can often experience a flood of emotions. Being aware that our emotions can produce conflict if we allow ourselves to act on them can help us avoid making decisions that create conflict. Before we expect others to understand how we feel, we can pause to consider why we feel as we do. By pausing to reflect on our feelings, we can also consider the feelings of others. Taking these moments allows us to avoid conflicts created by a flood of emotions.

Attention needs to be drawn to the role of religion, science and philosophy throughout history. Regardless of professions of faith, each belief system that exists attempts to give wisdom and understanding of how to attain the type of life we all desire through the choices we make.

Throughout history it has become apparent to people throughout the world that the conflicts which occur between groups and nations originate within the hearts and understanding of individuals. All belief systems place great importance on the actions we take matching a moral standard of thought we should all be conscious of in our daily lives. Like a river, our thoughts and emotions have a natural flow that swells when we are filled with feelings and can seem dry when we do not have what we feel we need. This quote directs our attention to how controlling our thoughts, actions and emotions goes beyond the natural flow of what we feel when we attempt to control ourselves as we interact with others.

HOW THIS APPLIES TO SELF AWARENESS:

At the time in history when the book of Proverbs was written, the science of agriculture and mass irrigation of crops to support large communities was very much in its developmental stages. At the time the development of reservoirs, control gates and canals to control water across vast distances was considered the height of human intellectual achievement and ability to control our environment to satisfy our needs.

When the author of the quote refers to the releasing of water, it is likely a reference to the actual operation of devices used to release water into irrigation systems. In these systems a gate to release water was often made of wood and in order to keep the canals and levies from collapsing it was best to open the gate slowly so as to avoid flooding the ground and destroying crops. It was also necessary to maintain the condition of the gates which could develop leaks resulting in overwatering of food sources or gates breaking which would result in no control or ability to save needed water. Even under controlled, properly operated and properly maintained conditions the flow of water into a field the understanding of how water flowed needed to be applied by the farmer. Even after the control gate was closed, water would continue to flow from the canal into the field. The control gate needed to be operated so that what was left over after closing it would not damage the crops.

Strife is that feeling we get when we know something needs to be addressed but has not yet turned into a conflict. Our emotions generally begin to build around a situation or circumstance between ourselves and some person place or thing. Our actions and ability to address a sense of strife within our emotions acts as a control gate to care for our happiness and well-being. By controlling whether or not our felling of strife turns into a flood of argument and conflict between ourselves and others we must give thought to how we express our emotions and how much. We must also look at the actions we take to maintain happiness and well-being for ourselves and others we care for. If what we choose to do or how we express ourselves causes regular conflict, the way we deal with our individual responsibilities is like a damaged control gate.

SELF AWARENESS

MODULE 4: LESSON 1

WHY DO WE FEEL CONFLICT AND ADVERSITY?

Situations that were once difficult become easier and we find new challenges as we grow older. As we are faced with meeting the responsibilities we are given, our individual attention to how we interact with others is not often a focus of our attention. Some individuals develop the ability to communicate in order to get what they want. Some people are never taught how to communicate their desires. Between these two levels of capability also exist a wide range of ideas each person can develop which define for them a belief of what is important for themselves and others. We become more accustomed to feeling adversity and conflict as we become more confident in our ability to address them. **However, our experiences addressing conflict and adversity do not necessarily mean we have learned to address them well.** Most of us realize the value of cooperating with others while some of us never see beyond what we want for ourselves or what we think we must do. As we grow we also become faced with the challenge of meeting new responsibilities while strongly focused on what we feel we should be able to do.

As we mature, each individuals feelings become attached to our ideas of what we want and how we think we can achieve our desires. We also begin to define ourselves by what we feel is right for ourselves and others. Often, it takes a larger amount of adversity for us to feel conflict. If everything we know how to do does not achieve what we want, our ability to resolve our desires becomes challenged in a greater way. If our ability becomes challenged by someone whose values we disagree with, our idea of what is right for ourselves and others may become challenged. We can feel challenged in both our abilities and identity of who we are. This makes conflicts seem larger as we grow older.

NOTES:____

Having established the principles that:

Our confidence and sense of identity which comes from our ability to do things can blind us to what we may not know.
Each person develops confidence and a sense of identity based in their individual experiences.
Our ability to examine ourselves and what we do directly effects the happiness and well-being we create for ourselves and others.

Areas of conflict and difficulty often arise out of what we prefer within any given circumstance rather than what is best for the situation. Whether or not we feel we are able to get what we prefer to happen or exist within a particular circumstance can frustrate our sense of Peace and Security. How well we can accept not getting what we want determines how much conflict arises out of our frustration.

TYPES OF DIFFICULTY & CONFLICT:

Embarrassment
Arguments
Repeated comments by others
Things that interfere with our abilities to do other things.

QUESTIONS:

1. Ask the student to describe something that causes conflict between themselves and someone they care about.
2. Ask the student what they wanted or chose to focus on as there preferred solution to the conflict.
3. Was there something other than what they preferred which could have provided peace and security for themselves and the other person.

One of the greatest personal challenges for many adults is understanding how to change our desires to include the concerns of others. We can often assume that what we feel is right for us must also be right for everyone.

EXAMPLE 1:

During High School, Billy's life always seemed busy and there never seemed enough time to do everything. Between school and home Billy would rush to do everything he needed to get done. When he was sixteen, Billy's mom asked him to drive his brother and sister to school and watch them until she got home from work. Billy's days were filled with, getting to classes on time, washing dishes from the last night's dinner and helping his siblings until his mom came home. Billy would do his homework while his mom cooked dinner and watch TV before going to sleep. Billy knew it was hard for his mom to work and take care of everything and he tried not to ask for a lot of things.

The week before High School prom, Billy's mom gave him a tuxedo to wear and a ticket to the dance. Even though Billy had not asked to go, his mom wanted to say thank you for the way he always helped her. Billy was happy his mom had thought of him and thanked her for the gifts but it made him nervous to think about going. Billy never took time do more than say a few words to the girls he liked. With only a week left, almost everyone who had tickets were already going with someone else. Billy didn't know who he could ask to go with him and felt bad thinking about going alone. Billy remembered his mom telling him he should go to the dance a few weeks earlier. Billy wished he would have told her he wanted to go.

NOTES: **PERSONAL EXPERIENCES**

We all form our abilities to deal with change but may not be aware of why we become frustrated or what we actually desire from life as we go through change. Much of our inner conflicts are not discussed with others because we may feel uncertain of our own thoughts about ourselves and not wish to be judged. We can often avoid things due to no other cause than a feeling of discomfort, fear of the unknown or simply giving ourselves an excuse not to address things we would prefer not to think about or believe we would enjoy. Two perspectives of how this difficulty can be viewed are presented in how Billy approaches his situation and in how Billy's mom responds to the situation. The perspective of a child learning as they mature is seen in Billy's decisions. The perspective of an understanding adult who has already experienced these difficulties and does not wish to allow something to exist as an excuse to Happiness, Well-being, Peace and Security for everyone involved.

OPPORTUNITY FOR DISCUSSION:

Many adults often behave no differently than when they were teenagers. When we look at the idea of the type of life we would like to live, we often do not consider the maturity it requires to have a larger life filled with lasting relationships. Whether or not we plan to have children, we become responsible for the well-being of others in all types of adult relationships. It is healthy to consider how much understanding we give the people we care for.

EXAMPLE 1 QUESTIONS:

1. Why do you think Billy did not tell his mom he wanted to go to the dance?______________________________

2. Do you think Billy had thought about going to the dance before his mom gave him a ticket to go?__

3. Do you think Billy's responsibilities were a good reason not to go or an excuse he used for not asking to go to the dance? ______________________________

CRITICAL THINKING:

1. Not including taking care of his siblings, what reason could Billy have for not telling his mom he wanted to go to the dance? What was the personal adversity he dealt with?______________________________

2. In a few words, describe the conflict Billy faced at the end of the example and how he helped create it._

NOTES: PERSONAL EXPERIENCES

There are no right or wrong answers to example 1 questions.

SUGGESTED ACTIVITY:

Discuss the students answers within the context of Example 1 opportunity for discussion.

QUESTIONS:

1. Could mom have ignored the issue?
2. Would you rather be the person who does not address issues or the person who makes an understanding decision and removes excuses for allowing difficulty and conflict to exist?
3. Are there any every day type of decisions or activities and tasks you avoid?

SELF AWARENESS

MODULE 4: LESSON 2

We often judge ourselves based on what we believe life is like for the people we see around us as we mature. Circumstances that seem to create adversities for us can often appear simple for others. Each of us feels this way about others when we see people doing things we would like to do but cannot understand how we would be successful. We often think having many similar circumstances means we should be able to do the same things. If this were true we would all be talented artists, musicians and athletes. We find it fairly easy to accept that we do not all share the same artistic or physical talents. However, we find it difficult to accept that we are different in other areas as well. **Each person has different adversities and conflicts which challenge them to change in order to remove difficulties from their lives.** Because we each have different experiences we also each have different difficulties and challenges. We all have challenges others may not and where we find life less challenging others may have difficulty.

As we reach an age when we begin interacting with others independently, circumstances require us to take action causing us to feel difficulty. From an early age we have developed expectations of others. We have relied on most of our needs being provided for us. The change in our responsibilities causes us to question how we can care for ourselves. Most of us feel ill-equipped to provide for ourselves during our youth. We do not have a sense of security in our ability to meet our needs. When what we expect from others becomes what we must do for ourselves; we can also feel mistreated. We often focus our discomfort facing the difficulties of responsibility on others. We may blame our parents, teachers and even our friends for what we feel is unfair. Our identity as a person who's' needs will be provided is being required to change. The peace we have felt within the security of being cared for is replaced with the adversity of caring for ourselves. By focusing our frustrations on others we create conflict between ourselves and others. **In order to avoid conflict we must be able question our abilities without creating conflict**.

NOTES: PERSONAL EXPERIENCES

____

____

____

____

____

____

____

____

____

Much adversity and conflict we feel is based not only our individual idea of who we are but also in how we compare ourselves to others. Comparing ourselves to others can cause us to feel there are things we should be able to do but lack knowledge, experience or ability to do them. We can find ourselves attempting to fit ourselves into an idea we have of what everyone's life should be like. We often ignore the difficulties of striving to achieve this idea as we attempt to make it a reality for ourselves. Doing this can cause us to find a level of success while having little or no happiness. Many adults never question the choices they make for themselves because we are all presented with an idea of how to care for ourselves by the example our parents provided. Whether or not the way we choose to achieve our success is supported by our talents, skills and personal beliefs is often never questioned. Most adults set out to establish satisfying their needs and desires for life doing what they have been taught. We hope to someday be able to express our talents, skills and personal beliefs once we become stable in providing for our basic needs. For many of us, the results is a sense of frustration that we will never reach a point where we can do what we really want because we are too busy meeting our basic needs. This frustration often turns to conflict between ourselves and the people we care for. We can build resentments that create conflicts because we never stopped to question and define our true abilities.

EXAMPLE 2:

It was senior year and Sally had done everything her parents asked of her all through high school. Sally had made good grades, she was Captain of the cheer squad, Treasurer of the Student Body Council, her applications to college had been accepted and she had a partial scholarship to a school her parents felt was not too far away. Sally had six months left before graduation and now her parents expected her to get a job.

"This is ridiculous", Sally told her friend. "I've worked hard and done everything I am supposed to. This is supposed to be my time to have fun with my friends before we all never see each other again". Sally picked up a couple of applications and decided to tell her parents why she did not think it was fair for them to make her get a job before graduation.

Sally knew her parents were always willing to talk things over and a couple days had gone by since Sally's parents had talked to her about getting a job. Sally felt she was doing well as she explained everything she was already doing and none of her friends were having to get jobs. Sally felt she made perfect sense when she explained the fact all of her friends were going to out of state colleges when she was going to a local college and how unreasonable it seemed to make her get a job.

Sally's face felt rushed, her hands tightened and she wanted to scream when her parents told her that they understood but if Sally wanted to be able to drive a car she would also need to get a job.

EXAMPLE 2 QUESTIONS:

1. Did Sally's thoughts and feelings about getting a job seem reasonable? Why?________________________________

2. Is it reasonable that a person needs to work in order to pay for driving a car? (Y/N)________

3. Do you think it would be impossible for Sally to have fun with her friends if she was working or if Sally did not know how she would be able to? Why?________________________

CRITICAL THINKING:

1. In your own words, explain the adversity Sally faced when she was told she needed to find a job.________________
____

2. Understanding how Sally felt at the end of the example: Explain in a few words how reacting on how she felt would turn the adversity Sally was facing into a conflict between herself and her parents.____________________________

Without being aware of our behavior, many of us respond to meeting new responsibilities without mature consideration of ourselves, the circumstances or how we relate ourselves to others. This is how everyone responds to new challenges in youth. In our youth we often assume that what we should or could do will be explained by someone else. That is what happened when we were children. Perhaps our parents did not know how to explain a process of facing challenges. Perhaps we stopped asking for advice because we assumed they did not know or decided not being told meant we had reached the end of their ability to help. In either situation, many adults decide there are things that everyone has to figure out for themselves. As youth we often become fixated on end results & imagined consequences of new responsibilities effecting what we want to do. We argue and grudgingly accept the realities of what is required to have independence. Without being aware of ourselves many of us carry this habit into adulthood. We then choose to do things because we have to and never consider how we can meet our responsibilities in a way that accommodates our desired results. We create conflict for ourselves and others by believing we are required to give up who we are. We often spend our lives resenting others for this when we can choose to examine and change our choices at any time.

SELF AWARENESS

MODULE 4: LESSON 2

TOPIC SUMMARY:

Much like any other activity that requires practice, we progress from a basic level through more complicated learning to become good at responding to adversity and conflict. **We must recognize for ourselves where we have difficulties and ask ourselves what we can do to resolve those difficulties.** Many of us do not like to think that we may be incapable of figuring out our own problems. Many of us are concerned with how others might view us if we admitted we need help to figure out solutions. The feeling of adversity is something each individual feels within themselves when facing a challenge. Conflict is the result of how we choose to respond to adversity. Each adversity we face is an opportunity to examine what we want from any given situation. **When we pause to consider what we want, what we can control and what we cannot change, we give ourselves the opportunity to avoid conflict.**

TOPIC ASSIGNMENT:

Write 3-5 paragraphs (3-5 sentences each) considering an event where you felt adversity, how your own decisions helped create conflict and describe what choices you could have made to avoid conflict.

It is impossible to examine every situation in which we might encounter adversity and conflict. In order to appropriately respond to adversity and conflict we must be able to recognize them as opportunities. We can act in ways to support the life we want to live. Adversity exists in simply looking at areas of our lives we need to improve. There is conflict we create for ourselves by judging ourselves or comparing ourselves with others. By accepting adversity as a challenge to mature, we remove the conflict we create by resisting change. By focusing on our Talents, Skills and Personal beliefs to assist us in facing adversity, life becomes what we are living rather than what we are required to do.

SUGGESTED ACTIVITY:

Before assigning the Topic assignment.

Review the personal goals the student outlined for themselves before beginning the training modules. Discuss the outlined goals asking the student to apply Module 4, Example 1, Question 2:

"Would you rather be the person who does not address issues or the person who makes an understanding decision and removes excuses for allowing difficulty and conflict to exist"?

REVIEWING TOPIC ASSIGNMENT:

Discuss with the student that there are no right or wrong answers to any of the training questions. Every answer given by describes our own beliefs on how to transition to adulthood. It is our choice to apply our beliefs or not to apply them. It is a choice to live as a contribution to life and the world around us.

Instructions for "BOLD REALITIES" section:

Bold Realities for Discussion are portions of the text which appear in **Bold Type** within the Training Module. It is suggested that the discussion of these principles be conducted in an informal manner. Discussing this portion casually reinforces the understanding of the subject material within the mind of the student. This forum allows that understanding to be freely expressed without the requirement of structured questions, answers or written assignments. It is suggested that each be discussed separately and within the context how they are combined.

BOLD REALITIES

FOR DISCUSSION

When a situation challenges our ideas and abilities we feel that our identity as a person is being challenged. In most cases our concern for ourselves centers in what we like or dislike. All adversity we feel results from what we focus on as our desires and challenges to our success in achieving what we desire.

Conflict arises when our ability to address adversity is challenged or seems completely ineffective. However, our experiences addressing conflict and adversity do not necessarily mean we have learned to address them well.

Each person has different adversities and conflicts which challenge them to change in order to remove difficulties from their lives. In order to avoid conflict we must be able question our abilities without creating conflict. We must recognize for ourselves where we have difficulties and ask ourselves what we can do to resolve those difficulties. When we pause to consider what we want, what we can control and what we cannot change, we give ourselves the opportunity to avoid conflict.

www.ingramcontent.com/pod-product-compliance
Lightning Source LLC
LaVergne TN
LVHW070153110826
845147LV00002B/390

* 9 7 8 0 5 7 8 4 7 0 2 6 9 *